D1496359

Dr. Melissa Sadin & Nathan Levy's

Teachers' Guide
to Trauma:
20 Things Kids with Trauma Wish
Their Teachers Knew

with Theo Sadin

A Nathan Levy Books LLC Publication

Copyright 2019

Revised

Nathan Levy Books, LLC
18 Moorland Boulevard
Monroe Township NJ 08831
www.storieswithholes.com
nlevy103@comcast.net

ISBN 978-0-9997908-1-6

Printed in the United States of America

Cover artwork by Dallin Orr
www.dallinorr.com

*This book is dedicated to Melissa's mother, Ann, Theo's grandmother, Mamie.
We love you. We thank you.
We miss you.*

Special thanks to Dominique Zuani-Levy for her help in producing this book.

We begin our trauma guide with Dr. Melissa Sadin and Theo's personal story. Theo's journey taught Melissa much about educating traumatized children. Let us hear Dr. Sadin give the background that has ultimately led to the wisdom that follows.

This book represents the sum total of all that I have learned loving and educating my son, Theo. Theo was born in Bulgaria and spent the first three years of his life in a Bulgarian orphanage. When we brought him home, he had no language. He was not even uttering the Bulgarian equivalent of "baba", "no," "yes" or "momma." He was brave, and he was funny. He worked very hard to understand me and the strange new world in which he found himself.

After Theo was home for three months, I enrolled him in pre-school. He needed peers, and I needed to return to my job as an assistant principal in an elementary school. And so began our 15-year journey to help teachers understand Theo and to help Theo learn. Looking back now, I realize that Theo was the teacher and we were all his students.

Preschool was hard for Theo. Every time I left him at the wonderful little preschool program we found for him, he believed he would never see me again. Every time I left him, his brain would replay the day his birth mother brought him to the orphanage. Of course, at the time, he could not tell us that. He would be distracted by the activities in his class for a while. Then the fear of abandonment would consume him, and he would rage. Sometimes for hours. His teachers were patient and kind. But they were not able to reduce the tantrums or predict when they would occur.

Theo's preschool experience repeated itself throughout his school years. He would hold it together until the experiences of his early childhood would overwhelm and consume him. He responded to teachers who "got him" and raged against teachers who did not. Theo is thankful to the teachers who "got him." He was most deeply affected by his middle school assistant principal, Mr. Reavey. Middle school is hard for most kids. Things that are hard for kids without trauma are infinitely harder for kids with trauma. But Mr. Reavey never gave up trying to understand Theo and provide an environment for him that would promote academic success. Theo and I have spent hours reflecting and discussing what teachers did that helped him and what teachers did that hurt him. Theo believes, as do I, that teachers who know better can do better. So, we give you this book in the hope that we can do better for the thousands of children in schools across the country who, like Theo, have developmental trauma.

Introduction

One in four children in every classroom, every day has experienced some type of trauma. Children who have prolonged exposure to trauma in childhood, including but not limited to family violence, physical, emotional or sexual abuse, separation from a primary care giver, and poverty are considered to have developmental trauma (DT). This type of trauma exposure may impair neurobiological development. The brains of children with prolonged trauma exposure may not be the same as children without trauma. Prolonged exposure to early childhood trauma causes atypical development of the amygdala, hippocampus, and prefrontal cortex. These important parts of our limbic system are necessary for, among other things, emotional control, language development, memory, and cognition.

In typical development, all children are amygdala driven at birth. The amygdala is also known as our survival brain. It is responsible for our survival behaviors. Human infants are completely unable to survive alone. If you put an infant in a field alone, eventually, he will die. Babies cannot keep themselves warm. They cannot feed themselves. They cannot drink by themselves. They need another human to provide their basic needs. The amygdala is what causes babies to cry. They cry when they are hot. They cry when they are cold. They cry when they are hungry. They cry when they are thirsty. They cry when they are afraid. They cry when they are lonely. They cry as a way to bring another human to help them. If you have ever raised a baby or been close to someone who has, then you know that it is a pretty good system. When a baby cries, we respond. We pick him up. We ask him, "What's wrong?" We hold him, bounce him, check his diaper, check the time to decide if he is hungry or thirsty. While we are going through our checklist of what might be wrong, very often we are telling him that he will be all right. We tell him, "It's okay." When we do this over and over thousands of times over 2 to 3 years, the amygdala responds less, and the hippocampus gets busy. The hippocampus is the center for things such as self-regulation, language development, and memory. The activity in the hippocampus helps us realize that every discomfort is not life threatening. We can be hungry. It is okay. We will get food soon. We are cold. It is okay. We can get a coat or move to a warmer place. We begin to do for ourselves what our parents did for us when we were infants. Over the next 10 to 15 years, when we continue to have a safe place where our basic needs are met, our pre-frontal cortex comes online. With the pre-frontal cortex comes delayed gratification, choice, empathy, reasoning, and judgement.

Children with trauma have atypical limbic system development. Often, they do not get their basic needs met as infants and babies and toddlers. Their amygdala remains in charge. They are constantly on alert for perceived threats to their safety. With recent medical advances and the development of the functional magnetic resonance imaging (fMRI) machine, neurobiologists, scientists, and medical doctors have been able to study the response centers in the brains of living human subjects without endangering the safety of the subject. Research shows that children with trauma often have larger amygdala and smaller hippocampus volume than children without trauma. It is important to understand that this means that children in a 5th grade class may have the pre-frontal cortex activity of a 4-year-old. High school students who have experienced trauma may have the judgement of a 5th grader. Brains cannot skip stages of development. A child cannot do more than their brain development allows. Children who are amygdala driven cannot choose their behavior. Sixteen-year-old young adults with DT may not choose a good peer group. They may not make age appropriate decisions while operating a vehicle.

They may not be able to wait their turn in class the way a child without trauma can.

Many children with trauma histories also have attachment disruption or disorganization as a result of absent or inconsistent care. Attachment occurs while we are picking our babies up, holding them, telling them they will be okay, and looking at them. Attachment develops when we stare forever, fascinated, by our babies' faces. Attachment happens when we feed our children dinner every night. Children with trauma may have intermittent experience with parental gazing. They may begin forming healthy attachment that is interrupted by a parent that is no longer physically or emotionally available. This results in delayed development of the internal working model (IWM). A functioning IWM is necessary for the development of trust. Establishing relationships is necessary for survival. Children with an impaired or absent IWM have difficulty establishing relationships and regulating behavior. They often have intense feelings of hopelessness. They experience extreme shame and they have no sense of self. This interferes with their ability to develop self-regulation, self-determination, and self-efficacy. *Self, self, self.* You need a self to develop any of these capacities. Children without an IWM have a skewed or absent sense of self. They cannot engage in self-talk.

Schools are largely cognitive behavioral systems. We teach children to make good choices. We ask them to identify their feelings and to develop strategies for replacing inappropriate behavior. Cognitive behavioral systems assume cognition and a sense of self. Children with developmental trauma often have limited cognition due to the impaired limbic system development and little or no sense of self. They are not ready for the cognitive behavioral systems present in schools. They cannot tell you how they are feeling, and they cannot choose to behave differently.

Imagine that schools are ponds. In the ponds are ducks. Ducks of many shapes and sizes. Ducks with autism. Ducks with dyslexia. We have become very good in this country at educating ducks. The problem is that in our ponds, among the ducks sit lions. Lions cannot be cared for the same way as you would care for a duck. They need different food and a different environment. If you leave a lion to be raised in a duck pond, she or he will do one of three things: *freeze* – stop trying to eat the duck food and eventually die; *flee* – leave the pond in search of tall grass and meat; or *fight* – eat the other ducks.

Educators need to shift their paradigm. They need to ask, "What's happened to you?" instead of "What's wrong with you?" Teachers need to see students who are not doing what they have been asked to do as students who cannot, not as students who will not. Doing so, teachers can help children with developmental trauma increase their pre-frontal cortex activity and strengthen their IWM. Children with developmental trauma need to feel safe -- safe from judgement, punishment, and misunderstanding. With unconditional acceptance, they learn to establish relationships. Teachers can help children develop the ability to regulate their emotions through the creation of personal connections. When children with developmental trauma feel safe, they begin to connect with teachers. Children who are safe and connected are ready to learn. Children who are ready to learn are increasing pre-frontal cortex activity.

Educators must understand that to respond in a trauma-informed way means that their students must feel safe and learn to regulate their emotions before they can learn. Asking children who do not have a properly developing pre-frontal cortex to choose better behavior is like asking a child without wings to fly. Asking children to pull themselves up by their boot straps when they do not even have boots will trigger their shame. They will feel unsafe and will take whatever steps are necessary to ensure their survival. This behavior is likely to be deemed inappropriate and subject to disciplinary action. Disciplinary action will exacerbate the intense shame and fear which will intensify the problem behavior.

As stated previously, in order to create schools where all students can learn, we need to shift our paradigm. We need to ask our students, "What's happened to you?" If almost half of the students in any classroom have a trauma history, then teachers should start with personal connections and very high acceptance. The best news is that children without trauma respond as well to personal connections and acceptance as children with trauma. Ducks do very well being raised as lions. If you treat all of your students as though they need acceptance and personal connections, they should all feel safe, learn to regulate their emotions and be available for learning. What follows are 20 things Theo, Nathan and I believe will help you shift your paradigm and improve the learning for all of your students.

Beyond Theo

    With Dr. Sadin's personal story in mind, we have combined our experiences and Dr. Sadin's research to put forth a practical trauma guide that should be useful to parents, educators (teachers & administrators) and counselors in their daily interactions with all children. For those who work with children with trauma, this guide should be even more essential. ***One size fits one***. With attention to our suggestions and Dr. Sadin's personal experience, we believe many traumatized children will be more productive students. Let us begin.

1

Do not yell at me – I fight, freeze or flee because the yelling triggers my amygdala.

A child with developmental trauma may have an amygdala that is larger than the amygdala of a child without trauma. The amygdala is our survival brain. It is the part of our brain that helps us flee a burning building or lift cars off babies. When babies are born, their behavior is driven by their amygdala. They are in survival mode. Babies cry when they are cold, hungry, or need connection with their parents. Over time, as their needs are met, they learn to soothe themselves. They become attached. They learn to trust that they will get their needs met. Children who do not get their basic needs met as infants and young children do not learn to soothe themselves. They cannot trust that their needs will be met. They remain in survival mode.

Children in school who perceive that a teacher or staff member is "yelling" at them will resort to one of the three survival responses: freeze, flight or fight. Students in a freeze response can look like they are not listening or attending to the teacher who is speaking to them. They do not answer questions that are asked of them in that moment. Students in a flight response will move away, leave the room, or ignore the teacher as they are walking past. Students in a fight response will defend themselves by any means necessary. They will talk back, yell back, throw things, curse, and/or punch.

Students with developmental trauma need teachers to remain calm and in control. When adults model calm and controlled behavior, children can feel safe. When a student needs correction, using blame free and positive language will reduce their shame trigger and help them to stay present in the situation. Balancing the individual needs of a traumatized child in turmoil with the safety of other class or family members can be challenging. Being firm and consistent are long standing maxims. Our recommended maxim is be firm, consistent, and caring.

Notes

2

Avoid Sarcasm – I have language processing issues and do not understand abstract words. I often assume you are making fun of me.

Prolonged exposure to early childhood trauma impairs development of the hippocampus. The hippocampus is responsible for memory, self-regulation, and language development and many other skills necessary for learning.

Have you ever learned to speak a language other than your native language? Or have you ever been in a place where many people around you are speaking a language you do not understand? While you are learning a new language, you speak very slowly because you are working to make sense of what was said to you, and it takes time to find the words to use to respond. Some children with developmental trauma are not fluent in their only language. The last piece to learning a new language is understanding humor, idioms, and sarcasm in the new language. Many children with developmental trauma never reach fluency and thus, do not understand idioms and sarcasm. They assume you are making fun of them. They can and should be taught idioms. Explaining what idioms mean can be helpful. Sarcasm is not clear. They are in survival mode. In the space of not knowing, they will assume the worst.

For children with developmental trauma and language difficulties, teachers should treat them as though they are not fluent in a language. Use concrete language. Avoid abstract terms. Give directions in writing. Show them more than tell them what you want them to learn.

<u>Coloring Page</u>

Illustration from the book "Whole Hearted, Whole-Brained Parenting" by Tiffany Junker. Illustrations by Rian Kasner.

3

Show me what I do well – I have a negative world view and am unable to see the good in myself.

Children who have attachment disruption often have a negative world view. Attachment can be disrupted by living with a parent whose care is inconsistent or consistently poor, or losing a parent through death or imprisonment, or living in an orphanage, or living in foster care. Children who are abandoned by their parents either intentionally or unintentionally often see themselves as less. They believe they are somehow at fault for the loss. It is important to note that this belief can be unconscious, especially if the loss or abandonment happened in early childhood. Children with this type of experience are unable to see what others may see as skill or talent. They may be gifted athletes who quit the sport. Or beautiful singers who refuse to perform. Talented musicians who will not practice. They may engage in their area of talent for a time. But they will often walk away from it. They believe that they are not really that good, and sooner or later everyone else will see that too. The "imposter syndrome" may take effect.

In addition, they cannot use their talent or skill to develop self-esteem. They can be popular in school and still report that they have no friends. In their minds, they are less. They are no good. They are disposable. They are not going to spend any time developing themselves, and therefore, you should not either.

Children with a negative world view need to be shown what they can do. If they are good students, show them the pattern of good grades. Talk to them about it. Ask them what they think. Set goals. Build on short term objectives that lead to goal attainment. Remember, they may not take a big risk by setting a goal they do not believe they can achieve. Start small. Ask them to complete one problem. Break big assignments into smaller parts. Avoid crossing off the ones they do not have to do. These kids have a negative view of themselves. If you cross off problems they do not have to do, they see it as confirmation that you think they are stupid, too. Be patient. Sometimes you may have to accept very small steps for weeks.

NOTES

4

*Learn about brain development then teach me about my brain – when I understand the way my brain has developed, then our conversations become about my brain and not about me.**

Children with developmental trauma have brains that are not often the same as children without DT. They have an over active amygdala and an underachieving hippocampus. They may have pre-frontal cortex activity that is years behind their actual chronological age. Research shows that with trauma-informed care, many children with DT can calm their amygdala and increase hippocampal and pre-frontal cortex activity. When you teach them explicitly about their brains, then you help them to understand that their struggles and challenges are not their fault. When you show them that their brains have plasticity, you give them hope where there was hopelessness. Children with developmental trauma must participate in their own healing. They are better participants when they understand why they are the way they are, and what they can do to improve it.

* A book called <u>Brain Whys</u> is a superior resource for this.

5

Help me out of my "Shame Cycle" – I get trapped in a loop and cannot get out on my own.

As shared previously, children with developmental trauma often have a negative world view. As such, they consciously or unconsciously believe that everything is their fault. This translates to intense, overwhelming, and often crippling shame. The shame loop looks something like this – The teacher sees Theo take a pen off her desk.

> Teacher: "Theo, that's my pen, please put it back."
>
> Theo: "What pen? This? This is my pen. I brought it from home."

He cannot admit that he took the pen because he cannot handle the shame of it. The teacher is likely feeling angry because Theo just lied to her face. The teacher may also feel hurt that Theo would take her belongings without regard to her feelings.

Children with DT often lie and steal. They often lie about what they stole and refuse to admit a lie even when the evidence is clear. They are also impulsive. They see something they want, and they take it. They are survivalists. They often do not possess the inner monologue that warns them if they take something that does not belong to them, they will get in trouble.

Think about a time when you messed up. Get in touch with how you felt when you had to confess. It is not a pleasant feeling. For children with trauma, that feeling is much more intense. So much so that it may threaten their sense of survival.

When working with a student with DT who lies or steals, come alongside them rather than confront them directly.

> Teacher: "Theo, next time you want to borrow my pen, just ask me."

Removing the shame from the behavior makes it safer for the student to return the stolen item. Detention is unlikely to get the lying and stealing to stop. After dealing with children in a shame free manner over time, they may develop trust and not feel the need to lie or steal.

A note about shame -- we can all get caught in a shame cycle. As you move through this guide, you may learn that things you have done in the past might not have been the best way to handle a student or a situation. It is important to remember that you do not know what you know until you know it. As you know better, you will do better. Let go of times you had an exchange or relationship with a student who may have been traumatized that you wish you could take back. There were many times that Dr. Sadin wishes she knew then what she knows now. All she could do was listen to Theo and learn as she went. That is all any of us can do.

COLORING PAGE

Illustration from the book "Whole Hearted, Whole-Brained Parenting" by Tiffany Junker. Illustrations by Rian Kasner.

6

Do NOT engage in a power struggle with me – I am a survivalist. I will hold onto the struggle like a dog with a bone and never let go.

A power struggle may look something like this. The teacher is sitting at her desk and sees Theo throw a paper ball at a classmate.

> Teacher: "Theo, why did you throw that at your classmate?"
>
> Theo with impunity: "What? Me? I didn't do anything."
>
> Teacher: "I saw you throw that paper. You need to pick it up and apologize to your classmate, or you will have to go see the principal."
>
> Theo: "I'm not picking it up because I didn't throw it. Whatever... You pick it up! It's your stupid classroom!"

Now he has insulted the teacher and challenged her authority. If the teacher holds her ground, Theo will eventually need to be removed. He cannot relent. It is not safe. His survival brain is in charge. If he backs down, he moves from predator to prey.

Teachers should stay out of the power struggle. Try to avoid threats. They only increase the challenge. Instead of tug-of-war, choose to walk alongside him. Try something like this…

> Teacher: "Theo, when you get a chance, can you throw that paper in the garbage?"
>
> Theo: "What paper? I didn't throw that. It's not mine." (He may not go right to insults like "your stupid classroom" if there is no threat in the initial statement.)
>
> Teacher: (Says nothing more; helps students with their work). At the end of class, very casually asks, "Hey, Theo can you get that paper for me?"

The request is cajoling and relationship building instead of threatening. Theo gets to make the decision. He perceives that he is still in charge. He remains predator and lives to learn another day. Detachment in your tone of voice does not mean detachment in your feelings or care for the student. Rather it may help your students feel calmer.

NOTES

7

*Take care of yourself – if you have a weakness physically or
emotionally, I will find it.*

Teachers need to be aware of their own adverse childhood
experiences (ACEs). Twenty years ago, Drs. Anda and Felitti
and their colleagues conducted a study. As a part of their
study, they surveyed 17,000 white middle class college
students. They asked them 10 questions regarding their
exposure to adverse childhood experiences such as physical
abuse, neglect, sexual abuse, domestic violence, substance
abuse in the home, etc. The results of the survey revealed that
as many as 64% of the population had experienced some type
of early childhood trauma.

Further research showed that people who have 3 or
more ACEs are at risk for poor adult health outcomes such as
cardiac difficulties, mental illness, life dissatisfaction,
hopelessness, cancer, and addiction. The survey they used is
known as the ACES survey. It is available online at
www.acestoohigh.com. Take the survey. Find out if you have
three or more adverse childhood experiences. If so, recognize
the impact your history has on your daily life. You may also
have a heightened stress response system. You may be a lion.

If so, you can easily be triggered by the behavior of other lions. Know when you need to walk away. Seek the support of your colleagues. Learn to understand that the frustration you may feel when working with some of your students with trauma is because your stress response system is being activated by your students.

As many as 46% of all teachers report high daily stress. That percentage is tied with reports from emergency room nurses. Teaching is stressful. Whether you work with a room full of traumatized students or you have one in your class, your job is stressful, and you need to take care of yourself. Exercise. Eat right. Get a massage. Go hiking. Make sure you employ the self-regulation activities that you teach your students. Learn to breathe. Use a pinwheel or glitter wand. Color during faculty meetings or at lunch. Make time for lunch. Make sure that you check in with yourself at least once during the school day.

COLORING PAGE

Illustration from the book "Whole Hearted, Whole-Brained
Parenting" by Tiffany Junker. Illustrations by Rian Kasner.

8

Teach me to self-regulate – give me a place to self-regulate.

When children have over active amygdala and a heightened stress response system, they need to learn to regulate these systems. Teachers need to learn about the limbic system and explicitly teach it to their students. When students understand why they lose their patience or become angry, they are better able to do something about it. There are some excellent resources out there to teach about the limbic system and provide suggestions for regulation activities. The *MindUp* curriculum provides developmentally appropriate lessons for K-2, 3-5, and 6-8 graders.

Create a space in the classroom for children to participate in regulation activities. A chill out space, keep calm corner, or place of peace can be created as needed. This space can be temporary or a permanent place in your classroom. Teach the children to use the space. The regulation space should be a place where children can go to actively work to regain control of their emotions. When children demonstrate the need for regulation, encourage them to consider going there.

You may notice that one of your students takes up residence in the place of peace. If you know this child has been exposed to trauma, make a plan to increase the time that the student is able to work in the general classroom space. Be patient. (There may be days that you want to take up residence in the place of peace. Try to keep those days to a minimum.)

Consider Iggy. Iggy came to kindergarten with a wonderful giggle and very little of anything else. As time went by, his teacher learned that he was living with his grandmother. His father was incarcerated, and his mother was gone. His grandmother loved him. He came to school clean and wearing appropriate clothing. In September, Iggy ran out of the classroom multiple times a week. Usually, when it was time for him to sit and engage in an assignment, he would laugh as he ran circles around the school. Sometimes he would take things off the bulletin boards as he ran by. He never tried to leave the building. His teacher put a plan in place with her principal, counselor and colleagues. When Iggy took off, someone would cover the class, and the teacher would go down the hall and let Iggy know she was there. She did not chase him, and she did not threaten him. She just stood at an intersection of the hallways so he could see her when he ran by. Then she would move down the hall toward her classroom when he was looking at her. He would run past and get to the classroom first or follow not very far behind.

Over time, Iggy would stand in the doorway when he became stressed, but he would not leave. He was becoming attached to his teacher. She became safe to him. Then the teacher set up a keep calm corner. Iggy moved in. He was in the corner all day, but he was not disrupting the class, picking on classmates or running out of the room. Once in a while, he would work one-on-one with the teacher on an assignment. Then, he began participating in class discussions from his corner. The teacher moved his guided reading group to a table next to the corner. Iggy was listening. He ended the school year spending half the day in the corner, and half the day with the class. He was much calmer. He was also on grade level in most academic areas.

9

Have an organized classroom – a disorganized classroom feeds my internal chaos.

Look at the physical arrangement of your classroom. Is there ample space to move around? Is there space for a keep calm corner or place of peace, if needed? There should be things on the walls that are directly related to the unit being studied. Are classroom rules posted? Is there a visible word wall? There should also be some empty space on the wall. Make sure the classroom materials are accessible to and appropriate for the students. A neat and organized space is a safe place for all children. A messy room feeds the chaos that is already present in the mind of a student with trauma. Middle and high schools should have spaces in the school for displaying student work so there is a sense of belonging and ownership for the students. All students can learn what exemplary models look like. The students (and adults) can and do learn by being exposed to excellence.

Notes

10

Establish a predictable and stable classroom community.

Routines are essential. Morning routines at home and in class allow children to know what to expect. For elementary school classrooms, post the daily schedule. Review it every day. For middle and high school classrooms, post the homework in the same place every day, even if you also put it in Google Classroom. Let children know when the schedule will change. If you know you will be out, try to arrange for the same substitute every time. Often, children with trauma have difficulty accepting substitute teachers. They have difficulty trusting and feeling safe with people. Substitutes are strangers. Children with trauma may move into survival mode in the presence of a substitute teacher. They might be rude or behave in unsafe ways. When they do this, they will usually be sent out of the room by the substitute teacher. That is what they wanted or needed in the first place, but lacked the ability to ask. Be proactive. In some cases, you may need to arrange for an alternative placement for a student for a day you will be absent. Middle and high school students can go to the counselor's office or the guidance office (a supervised. place where they are relatively familiar and comfortable). Elementary school students can spend the day with a teacher they know and trust. Focus on prevention.

Specifically communicate each day what the schedule will be. Post the schedule on the wall and tell your students. In middle school, if you have a high concentration of lions, consider creating a homeroom period where teachers have an opportunity to run a morning meeting. For high school, a 5-minute check-in before commencing learning activities can be very helpful to students with trauma.

Coloring Page

Illustration from the book "Whole Hearted, Whole-Brained Parenting" by Tiffany Junker. Illustrations by Rian Kasner.

11

Be consistent and fair with me.

Say what you will do, and do what you say. A good rule of thumb for superior teachers is to tell children what they are going to learn. Teach them. Tell them what they learned. Even better, have them tell you what they learned! Your lessons should follow the same pattern. I do, we do, you do. Introduce the content. Tell the students what the objective for the lesson is. Connect the day's lesson to previous learning. Allow the students to tell you how the new material might be connected. Ask questions. Connect the learning to your students. Encourage them to make personal connections. Follow this pattern for most lessons. Ask for quiet or attention the same way with words and hand signals.

Fair is getting what you need. Fair is not everyone getting the same thing. *One size fits one*. Teach your students about fair. Show them when it is applied. Being consistent and fair does not mean that you must respond the same way to all behavior.

NOTES

12

Teach me to dance - I do not hear the same relationship music. I am out of sync. Teach me give and take, the dance of attachment.

Parents are the primary attachment figures for children, but teachers, by virtue of spending several hours a day with their students, are certainly secondary attachment figures. This does not mean that teachers need to be the parent for all of their students. It means that they may participate in the instruction of relationship development for your students.

All children need to learn the give and take of relationships. I am honest with you, you are honest with me. I treat you with respect and you treat me with respect.

Attachment and the development of a relationship are like a dance. When you are attached to someone, you hear the same music. You move to the same beat. Children with trauma histories often do not hear the same music that children without trauma do. Imagine trying to dance with someone who is listening to very different music than you. The movements will not match. You may step on each other's toes. You will likely become so frustrated that you may give up and walk away.

Dr. Sadin's husband, Andrew, struggled with the idea of cause and effect, or more specifically, crime and punishment when Theo was young. He had a very hard time understanding why Theo was not punished in a traditional way when he made a mistake, hurt someone's feelings, broke a house rule, or damaged things in the house. Like many dads, Andrew was heard to say, "When I was a boy..." Andrew had to be reminded that he was not the same boy that Theo was. He did not spend the first three years of his life in an orphanage. One night, Melissa asked him to put on his headphones and play a song from his phone. (He is a big heavy metal fan.) He picked a Metallica song. Melissa put on headphones and picked her favorite song at the time, "The Greatest Love of All" by Whitney Houston. Then she asked her husband to dance with her. They could not find a common groove. Dr. Sadin explained that he needed to show her what he wanted her to do. An excellent dancer, Andrew persevered, and Melissa began to follow his lead. Eventually she was no longer listening to Whitney and was focusing on following him. They turned off their music, and she told him that his son needed Dad to teach him to dance. The relationship between father and son improved dramatically.

Think of your students as listening to different music. Teach them to have a relationship with you. Point out the things you do that show you care. Be honest. You can tell them when they are making you angry. Many students will soon model your dance. They will tell you how they are feeling. Be consistent. Use repetition.

13

Help me develop executive functions – I struggle to organize my approach to an assignment, and I lose everything that is not taped to my head.

Intelligence is considered the capacity to learn from experience using metacognitive processes to enhance learning and the ability to adapt to the surrounding environment. (Sternberg, 2005). Metacognitive in this case means the ability to think about thinking. It is a completely cognitive function requiring pre-frontal cortex activity. In addition, according to Sternberg, the ability to adapt to one's surroundings indicates intelligence. If you compare the ability of an 8th grader without trauma to think about thinking and to adapt to his surroundings with the ability of an 8th grader with trauma, it is likely that the 8th grader with trauma would come up lacking.

Our brain development cannot skip stages. If a child does not get sufficient opportunity for attachment and care in the early years, development in the hippocampus and pre-frontal cortex can be stalled. Therefore, an 8th grader with a trauma history may have the metacognitive ability of a 5th grader because that is where his brain development is.

Trauma-informed education is creating opportunities in school for brain development. This can be done by employing all of the strategies already covered in this book such as self-regulation, creating a feeling of safety, establishing trusting relationships, and teaching your students to think.

Executive functions are the skills required to conspire together to create metacognition, skills including auditory processing, memory, planning, language processing, logic and reasoning, visual processing, and comprehension. These skills are needed to assist students in everything we ask them to do in school. They need memory to follow two-step directions and to retain new content. They need planning to organize their learning material and to plan their approach to a task. They need attention to focus on a task and to persevere through a task. They need logic and reasoning to know what to ask about what they do not understand.

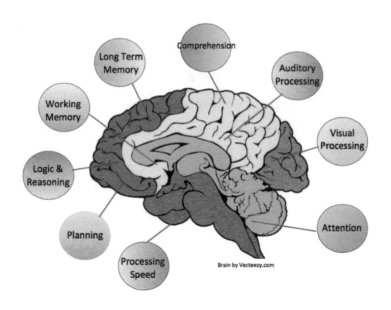

Brain by Vecteezy.com

Many children with developmental trauma, as a result of delayed limbic system development, have sporadic access to their executive functions. Some students with DT may have excellent memory and not be able to find anything the minute they take their eyes off it. Some students have impaired language development and struggle to understand the meaning of your spoken words. Children with auditory processing delays take a long time to make meaning of your spoken word and often to construct a response. These children can be accused of not listening. Take care with your lions. They may be listening, but without essential executive functions, they cannot do anything with the information they are listening to.

Teach your students to think. In elementary school, model how you want your students to come into the room and unpack. Show them and tell them. Let them practice. This is also an excellent opportunity for data collection. While they are practicing, you will quickly see who needs reteaching and repetition.

In middle school, teach how to maintain an organized locker. Show them when you tell them. Have locker clean out weekly in the beginning of the year. Help them learn to keep papers and books organized.

In high school, the children who forget to do homework, struggle to keep track of assignments, and lose things need explicit instruction. We have heard high school teachers say "Well, she should know how to do it. This is high school." The reply, "In a perfect world, you are correct." However, *one size fits one*. Our brains all develop at their own rate. Students with trauma have events that impeded their brain development. They are not the same as those without trauma. They can only use the parts of the brain that have developed. Reach them where they are. Back up as far as you need to find where they are functioning, and start from there. This instruction will benefit students without trauma as well.

There is an assessment for executive function called the BRIEF – Behavior Rating Inventory of Executive Function. In some states and in some districts, parent permission is required to administer the BRIEF. Check with your district's Student Services Director, Special Education Director, or someone who might know.

Coloring Page

Illustration from the book "Whole Hearted, Whole-Brained Parenting" by Tiffany Junker. Illustrations by Rian Kasner.

14

Be careful with homework – I may not have a safe place at home to work on school work. I may not remember what we did in school even if I seemed to understand it when we completed the sample problems.

Children with developmental trauma are often hyper-vigilant – ever alert for threats to their safety. Basically, they are distracted by survival. Have you ever experienced a trauma? If you have been in a car accident, you may be able to recall how you felt at the moment of impact. Your heart might have been pounding. Your ears may have been ringing. Your stress response system was in over drive. Your amygdala was activated. You were flooded with adrenaline and other stress response hormones. Imagine feeling that way in the middle of a math class. It would be very hard to concentrate. Even when children with trauma appear to be paying attention, they can be hijacked by their stress response system. They can come in and out of being present in the lesson. They may not even be aware this is happening.

In addition, prolonged exposure to early childhood trauma can impair working and short-term memory. Working memory is what we use when someone gives us a phone number. We may repeat it out loud or have the person repeat it so we can hold on to the information while we log into our phones to type it in.

Short-term memory is where we store information we use a few times or hold onto to pass the test, but do not remember a week or a month later. Children with developmental trauma need to be physically engaged in the learning, have the learning connected to their personal experience, or be involved in much repetition to move information from working memory to short term memory and eventually to long term memory. .It is common for children with developmental trauma to get home and not remember what they were working on in class even if they were able to complete the activity during independent practice. Parents may need to reteach. However, they were not present during the original instruction and cannot possibly repeat the lesson in the same way using the same vocabulary. For other children, their homes do not support the consistent completion of homework. They may not be safe, or the adults in the home may not value the completion of school work by providing an appropriate space or allowing time.

One size fits one. If a student is consistently missing homework, look into what might be in the way. Change the assignment to fit the student. Provide a place and time in the school at the end of the day for homework completion.

15

Lighten up – even when I am pushing your buttons. If you can stay light, it will relax my fear response.

Of all lessons I learned from Theo and other traumatized children, this may be the hardest. When children interrupt a lesson by calling out, challenging our authority, failing to comply with directions, we sometimes get angry. Sometimes we get our feelings hurt. After all, we prepared this lesson with care and deep consideration for our students. Sometimes a student's inability to participate in the lesson, especially if this student does this frequently, creates an emotional response in us. It is very difficult to remain detached, calm, and collected when our feelings are hurt, or we are angry. However, for our students with trauma, staying calm and holding on to a sense of humor can be a very powerful tool.

There was once a student, we will call him Wilson, who struggled with his behavior in the lunch room. Wilson was in middle school when Dr. Sadin worked with him. He was new to the school and was having a tough time adjusting. The lunchroom was a loud place teeming with organized chaos. About three days each week, Wilson would cause a significant disruption in the lunchroom. He would stand up, knocking over his chair in the process, and/or challenge a fellow student. Or he would punch the Snapple machine. Melissa heard about this behavior but had not witnessed it. One day, she was called to the lunchroom to meet Wilson. He was standing by the Snapple machine (which was already broken and had caution tape around it) with a chair up over his head. She walked up beside him and said, "Having a tough day?" With the chair still up over his head he looked over at her. Then he looked back at the Snapple machine and said, "Yeah." She said, "Me too. I was hoping to have a Snapple today." Wilson replied, "Too bad. It's broken." Melissa told him she was aware that the machine was broken. Slowly he put the chair down. She asked him if he liked Snapple. He smiled and said, "Actually, I do." She invited him to walk with her, and they left the lunch room. They talked a bit about what had made him so angry. It was a lot of things Dr. Sadin really could not change for him in a day. He was having problems with peers. He was having trouble with his school work. He was also very willing to tell her that it was everyone else's fault. She circled back to the Snapple machine. They decided together that maybe the lunch room was not a successful place for him right now. They made a plan for him to visit her the next day during lunch. After a few days of eating lunch together, Wilson and Dr. Sadin made a plan for Wilson to earn money to repair the Snapple machine. He never punched the machine again. Other things were done for Wilson. He met with the counselor a day or two a week during lunch for about two months. He was taught to get in touch with the dysregulation he felt in the loud, busy lunch room. Wilson returned to the lunch room after a few months and never had another outburst. Melissa says, "It was scary to walk up next to him. My heart was pounding. It is very difficult for most of us to be light or tell a joke when we are angry or frightened. Wilson shifted out of his hyper arousal because I approached him with the calm and sense of humor he was sorely lacking at the moment. We laughed a lot on our walk that day. Just because we laughed does not mean that he was not going to be held accountable. I could have scolded Wilson. He could have been given a speech about respecting property and all the school rules he broke. I chose to diffuse him and help him fix what he broke."

Coloring Page

Illustration from the book "Whole Hearted, Whole-Brained Parenting" by Tiffany Junker. Illustrations by Rian Kasner.

16

Be curious about me – ask me about what I like and what I am interested in.

Use my interests to engage me in learning. Being curious about students is good for all. We all like it when people are curious about us. "How are your children?" "Did you have a nice weekend?"

Being curious about your students with trauma will benefit the child in a number of ways. Asking them about themselves, what they like, why they seem upset, will often spark conversations that can assist in relationship development. Curiosity about them can help them feel acceptance which may lead to trust. When you have an established relationship of trust and acceptance with a child with trauma, you will have much more success helping that student learn to regulate and persist in learning.

Think about Freud's Id, Ego, and Superego. Freud believed that human development could be defined in three stages. Id is the first stage. In this stage, people are very self-centered. They are impulsive. They put their needs first. Ego is the next stage. In this stage, people have empathy. They are able to consider how their actions might impact others.

They are reasonable. Superego, the final stage, is characterized by altruism and conscience. Now think about what you have learned in this book about the limbic system. When children are amygdala driven, they are impulsive. They are unable to think about the feeling of others before acting. As the hippocampus develops, children develop the ability to self-regulate. They can soothe themselves. When the pre-frontal cortex comes online, children start to show the ability to think before they act. They think about the feelings of others. As the pre-frontal cortex develops, young adults are able to put themselves in the shoes of other.

If we loosely apply what we know about Freud's stages of development to what we know about limbic system development, we can understand why being curious about kids with trauma is helpful. We are developing relationships. Modeling the dance of attachment. Showing them how to care about others.

Remember Wilson. Dr. Sadin was curious. She asked him if he was angry. She had no prior relationship with Wilson. She connected quickly during their walk. Melissa used her curiosity to eventually get Wilson to do what she needed. She needed him to stop attacking the Snapple machine and to improve his overall behavior in the lunchroom.

17

Less is more – speak less, mean more. If you use too many words, I will lose or confuse your meaning. Then I become afraid and I will freeze, flee, or fight.

As we have learned, many children with developmental trauma struggle with language. For students with trauma who do not seem to be listening, cannot remember new material, or follow multi-step directions, consider that they may have unrecognized language development challenges. They may struggle to make sense of the words. They may take time to make meaning of the words (receptive language). They may also have trouble finding the words they want to use to say what they are thinking (expressive language). These students might need you to repeat things frequently.

Think of language development as a room filled with filing cabinets. As words are learned (receptive language), they are stored in the correct file with appropriate connections. When a child learns yellow, they connect yellow to the sun. So, the word yellow can be found under color and also the sun. Later the child learns the word raincoat. They may also learn that raincoats can be yellow. Connections are made.

When a child communicates with words (expressive language), she accesses her files and can find the words she wants to use when the teacher points to a yellow ball and asks what color it is.

Children with trauma may have a room full of half empty file cabinets with papers all over the floor and hanging out of drawers. They may not be able to file the word correctly, or they may not be able to find the word when they need it. As you can imagine, this gets very tiring so many children with this type of challenge give up. They start shrugging their shoulders in an "I don't know" gesture when called on in class.

Dr. Sadin calls them the "*Wait. What?*" kids. You are moving along in your lesson. You have visuals on the board. You might even be modeling a skill. When you check for understanding or send the class off for independent practice, your lion says, "Wait. What?"

Consider thinking about your students with language processing challenges as dual language learners. You can use this with all of your students with unique learning abilities, whether they have trauma or not. Think about them as though they have been in this country for a month. They are just learning the language, so their vocabulary is limited. You may have experience with dual language learners in your class. You use very concrete words. You show as much as you say. You constantly check for understanding. Use all of these strategies for any child who is struggling to understand what the words you say mean.

Please note: There are limited occasions and places in school for sarcasm. Keep your humor gentle until you know the child or adult well.

NOTES

18

Do NOT use point systems – class wide point systems make me feel defeated. Individual point systems are very threatening to me.

Students with trauma often have a negative world view. Essentially that means that they have trouble seeing the good in things, especially themselves. Often children with trauma have a sense that the trauma they suffered is somehow their fault, that they deserve it. It is the lens through which they see everything else. Dr. Sadin tells the following story about her son Theo:

"When Theo was about 4 years old, he decided that his favorite activity was pulling on my drapes. They were elaborate things with rigging, cords, and hundreds of dollars of material. He would walk over to them, grab a hold, and pull. If I walked into the room, he would smile. (I later learned that a smile in that setting is known as the orphanage smile. Often, children who spend time in an orphanage will smile when they are feeling uncomfortable, scared, worried, or threatened.) I went through all of the traditional responses one would use with a young child who pulls on drapes. "Mommy doesn't want you to pull in her drapes,' said while gently removing his hand from the drapes. Then, "Theo, stop pulling on the drapes." Then, "Theo, if you pull on those drapes one more time, you will go to time out." Then, on recommendation from my neighbor who was a very good mom to four children, "Hey, Theo, look at this shiny object over here away from the drapes." Nothing worked.

I spent many years as a special education teacher in a self-contained class for children with emotional/behavioral concerns. At the time, I was an assistant principal. I was an expert at behavior modification. I did workshops on classroom behavior modification systems. So, I cut a piece of construction paper in half. Theo, of course, picked out the color. I purchased large stickers, which Theo picked out. I explained in simple language that I would give Theo a sticker to put on the paper when he did what he was supposed to do. When he filled the paper with stickers, we would go to the dollar store and pick out a prize. We taped the paper to the fridge near the bottom where he could reach. We practiced. He put away his toys, I gave him a sticker. He put his clothes in the hamper, I gave him a sticker. A few days later, he was back to pulling on the drapes. I went through my repertoire. I added the sticker chart to the repertoire and told him that he would get a sticker if he stopped puling on the drapes. He pulled on the drapes. He pulled really hard on the drapes. I became worried that the rigging for the drapes would come out of the wall and fall on his head. He kept pulling. At this point, I was so angry that I walked away. This is not recommended as he could have gotten very hurt. But I was pushed past my limit. I went into the kitchen to pour some coffee, and I heard a crash from the other room. I went in and he was standing there with the curtains at his feet unharmed. A few minutes later he went into the kitchen with a sticker and said, "Mommy, I do?" I said, "No. No you don't". He looked up at me. Scrunched up his little face. Pulled the sticker chart off the refrigerator. Put it in his mouth, chewed it and swallowed. There was a minute where I worried about the amount of glue he had just ingested and whether that was good for him. My next thought was, "I'm going to need a new plan."

Theo's pulling on the drapes was the result of dis-regulation. He wanted to engage with her and had no model for doing that. He did not hear the same music his mother did. There were many reasons why he pulled those drapes off the wall. None of those reasons was that he wanted to hurt Melissa or make her angry. It was not about her. He was a long way from understanding her feelings and that he had some control over them. Pulling on the drapes was not a choice. As such, he was unable to choose not to pull on them so that he could get a sticker.

Theo's middle school had a school wide behavior plan. Students would earn points for breaking school rules. At certain levels of points, students would lose access to extra-curricular activities, field trips, etc. They could also be suspended or serve detention. In addition, students could earn tickets for prizes for demonstrating excellent academic performance, consistent attendance, and going point free for a semester.

In the middle of sixth grade, Theo earned some points for talking disrespectfully to his teacher. When the teacher told him that he would be earning discipline points for his behavior, he proceeded to tell her where she could go, how she could go, in what fashion she could go there. The teacher informed him that he had just earned more points. This might have gone on indefinitely. Thankfully, the assistant principal came along and escorted Theo to his office. He told Mr. Reavey he thought the points system was stupid and that, of course, it was not fair. When he came home he was very upset. He told me that he was going to earn more points than anyone in history of the middle school.

Theo was threatened by the point system. He was so sure that he would keep getting points that he made sure he was in charge of the points by racking them up on his terms. His feelings of worthlessness interfered with his ability to be motivated toward appropriate behavior to avoid points. When he became upset with his teacher or the school work, or his peers, he would become dis-regulated. He was amygdala driven. The possibility of failing with the point system created the same level of fear that a person without trauma feels when they are falling out of a window.

Dr. Sadin sent an email to Mr. Reavey explaining that they might need to find another way. She told Mr. Reavey about the drape incident. She explained that Theo would be more likely to participate in the point system or at the very least, not ruin his middle school career, by proving the system wrong, if he could fix what he broke. Mr. Reavey and Theo created a plan where Theo could erase points for positive behavior in school. The plan improved Theo's behavior. He had a few more missteps and one more attempt at being the high scorer for the school point system, but Mr. Reavey hung in there with him. They developed a bond. By 8th grade, Theo had very few points and was a fairly positive member of the school community.

Coloring Page

Illustration from the book "Whole Hearted, Whole-Brained Parenting" by Tiffany Junker. Illustrations by Rian Kasner.

19

I need help making choices regarding my behavior – if you teach me to self-regulate, I will build cognitive capacity and connections in my pre-frontal cortex. After time and when I am safe with you, I will be ready to learn how to make choices.

We have talked around this issue throughout this book. It is time to look directly at it. Children with DT have varying ability to choose. The ability to choose our behavior, to delay our gratification, to move from Id to Ego, requires capacity in our pre-frontal cortex. Children with DT may have limited activity in their pre-frontal cortex. They often have extensive activity in their amygdala and some activity in the hippocampus.

As mentioned in the introduction, schools are largely cognitive behavioral institutions built on social learning theory. Starting in kindergarten, students are taught to make good choices. Many schools administer elaborate character development programs throughout elementary school and middle school. However, one in four children in every class may not have the pre-frontal cortex development to make choices. They might model your behavior, but they cannot own it. Incorporating the self-regulation strategies covered in number 8 will help students develop their limbic system. Students will learn to regulate, and then they will learn to choose.

Remember, children cannot do more than their brains are ready for. They cannot choose until they can regulate. We believe that character development is important. Social emotional development is important. Teaching children to regulate should come before and be threaded through character development and social emotional development programs. Reading to kids is also important. Combine the two. Use literature to allow students to role play. They can take the part of a character that has skills that the student is working to develop. This has proven effective in changing behaviors and attitudes in positive ways.

NOTES

20

DO NOT suspend me or give me detention – I already feel worthless. If you suspend me, you are throwing me away. If you give me detention you prove me right.

Zero Tolerance came to schools from the federal government in response to the shooting at Columbine High School. Two students killed 12 and injured 21 people when they opened fire in their school. People were understandably scared. They wanted to be sure that their children would be safe in school. The message handed down from the federal government to administrators in schools across the country was protect the students at all costs. Boards of Education used language in their discipline policy that required administrators to remove students who interfered with the learning of others. Administrators at the time were told to suspend a 5-year-olds for making a gun symbol with their thumb and forefinger because it was a threat.

Much research has been conducted since Zero Tolerance was put into place. None of it shows that suspension makes schools safer. There is extensive research on the harm of suspension on children (all children). Study upon study shows that a child suspended in ninth grade is more likely to be suspended again. Children suspended more than once in high school are more likely to fail a grade and/or drop out. There is no evidence that suspensions improve behavior. There is evidence that children in schools where suspensions have been stopped feel safer in their school than children in schools where suspensions are still taking place.

For a student with trauma, suspension can be re-traumatizing. Students with DT may already feel thrown away or abandoned. Suspension and detention will heighten those feelings. We need to heal children, not punish them. Remember Wilson. If he had been suspended, would he stop attacking the Snapple machine? Our experience tells us that he would not.

Schools should find other ways to respond to behavior that interferes with learning. Find ways to help them fix what they broke. Help them find an action that communicates their apology. They will learn from this. They will grow their brain. They will be more likely to heal than go from high school to juvenile detention.

Important Note: Children who bring weapons and drugs to school should be removed for their safety and the safety of others. Hopefully, immediately following the removal of a student from the premises for weapons or drugs, the school contacts appropriate social services and provides wrap around services. A student who brings weapons or drugs to school is in pain. They are asking for help. Schools are full of people who can help them. Finding the line between what keeps people safe and criminal behavior is essential. Let us get better at recognizing children who hurt before they hurt others. But we must be willing to work with law enforcement when individuals or groups present life threatening behaviors to others.

Predictions

The future is here and coming at the same time. In helping veterans of World War I, World War II, and Vietnam, we learned about Post-traumatic Stress Syndrome (PTSD). This term was used to refer to the trauma faced by soldiers and civilians involved in war. We now know that PTSD is an adult diagnosis. Developmental Trauma is the term now used to describe children who have been exposed to war and other adverse childhood experiences.

What is coming are the same dangers we have faced with the expansion of special education, managing allergies, bullying, and other impediments to learning. Successful teachers and administrators must remember that the most important purpose of schools is to focus on student learning. . Student learning *and* safety, not one or the other. We cannot label children and consider them healed. We must do the teaching necessary. That is the future we must face together. We can succeed. We know better and are doing better. Let us keep improving our ability to reach all levels of learners – from children to adults. School shootings in Columbine High School, Sandy Hook Elementary School, and Stoneman Douglas High School in Parkland, Florida make the need for this work drastically evident.

Definitions

Amygdala – A physical part of the brain that is often referred to as the survival brain. Part of the limbic system often over developed in children with trauma.

Attachment - An emotional bond between an infant or toddler and primary caregiver. This strong bond is essential for the child's normal behavioral and social development.

Classroom Community – The people in the classroom and their connection to each other. Also, classroom structure, roles, responsibilities, and organization.

Developmental Trauma – Prolonged childhood exposure to any of the following: physical abuse, sexual abuse, emotional abuse, neglect, domestic violence, poverty, war, and separation from a primary care giver.

Executive Function - Set of processes that all have to do with managing oneself and one's resources in order to achieve a goal. It is an umbrella term for the neurologically-based skills involving mental control and self-regulation.

Hippocampus – Part of the limbic system in the mid-brain. Often under developed in children with trauma. Responsible for language, memory, and self-regulation.

Internal Working Model – A cognitive framework comprising mental representations for understanding the world, self, and others.

Pre-frontal Cortex – Part of the limbic system. Often under developed in children with trauma. Responsible for logic, reasoning, and processing speed.

Power Struggle – One of the ways that I feel safe is to try to control my environment. In a classroom or a house, that means being the boss of you. I feel it is too unsafe to let myself be controlled by you.

Self-Regulation – Calming of the stress response system through the use of strategies designed to move activity in the brain away from the amygdala and toward the pre-frontal cortex through the hippocampus.

Shame Cycle – I feel hopeless and unworthy. Since I am no good, I will make sure no one threatens me by acting out or being withdrawn. When I act out or withdraw, I feel even more unworthy. So, I act out or withdraw more. Children with trauma may need to be taught to break this cycle.

Toxic Shame – Overwhelming feeling of hopelessness common in child with trauma due to the toxic levels of cortisol and adrenaline produced because of the over active amygdala.

Sadinisms

1. You don't know what you don't know until you know it.
2. One size fits one.
3. When teachers know better, they do better.
4. Ducks who are raised as lions grow to be rock star ducks.
5. People with trauma have brains that are different than people without trauma.
6. Teaching is half science and half art. That's why you will not get the same answer for every problem.

Levyisms

1. Nothing done once works.

2. Things take time.

3. When children accomplish something they believe is difficult, self-esteem improves.

4. We imprint at an early age.

5. A. Early success is good for children's growth.

   B. Early failure in environments where the failure is ultimately overcome is also good for children's growth. (Some people now call this the growth mindset)

6. Active engagement is an important key.

7. Get children to engage and then make connections to curriculum or bigger ideas.

8. Children are not so different "nowadays". They need motivation and relevant teaching as they always have in a world that is becoming more and more complex for all of us.

Melissa and Nathanisms

1. Superior teaching addresses many of the needs of traumatized kids.

2. People with the same brain scans may behave vastly differently.

3. We all wish we could scan children's brains and know how to reach them. We can't. Even if we could see the scans, one size fits one.

4. A diagnosis or label can give us a direction to go or a lens through which to look, but it cannot guarantee results.

.

References

Adderholdt, M., Johnson, D., Levy, N. (2016). *Perfectionism vs. The Pursuit of Excellence-What Can Be Bad About Being Too Good.* New Jersey: Nathan Levy Books, LLC.

Anda, R.F., Butchart, A., Felitti, V.J., & Brown, D.W. (2010). Current issue: Building a Framework for Global Surveillance of the Public Health Implications of Adverse Childhood Experiences. *American Journal of Preventive Medicine*, 3993-98.

Attachment & Trauma Network (2016).

Fabelo, T., Thompson, M.D., Plotkin, M., Carmichael, D., Marchbanks, M.P.III, Booth, E.A. (2011). Breaking schools' rules: A statewide study of how school discipline relates to students' success and juvenile justice involvement. Council of State Governments Justice Center: New York.

Hanson, J. L., Nacewicz, B. M., Sutterer, M. J., Cayo, A. A., Schaefer, S. M., Rudolph, K. D., & ... Davidson, R. J. (2015). Behavioral problems after early life stress: Contributions of the hippocampus and amygdala. Biological Psychiatry, 77(4), 314-323.

Kochanska, Grazyna; Kim, Sanghag (2013). "Early Attachment Organization with Both Parents and Future Behavior Problems: From Infancy to Middle Childhood". Child Development, 84 (1): 283–296.

Molsbee, S. (2008). Zeroing Out Zero Tolerance: Eliminating Zero Tolerance Policies in Texas Schools, Texas Tech Law Review, 40, 325–334.

Moretz, C., Sears, P., & Levy, N. (2018). *Brain Whys*. New Jersey: Nathan Levy Books, LLC.

Siegel, D.J. (2012). The Developing Mind: How Relationships and the Brain Interact to Shape Who We Are. 2nd ed. New York: Guilford.

Substance Abuse and Mental Health Services Administration. (2014). SAMHSA's concept of trauma and guidance for a trauma— informed approach. HHS Publication No. (SMA) 14-4884. Rockville, MD: Substance Abuse and Mental Health Services Administration.

van der Kolk, B.A.(2005). Developmental Trauma Disorder: Toward a rational diagnosis for children with complex trauma histories. *Psychiatric Annuls, 35(5),* 401-409.

Melissa Sadin, Ed.D.

Executive Director: Ducks & Lions: Trauma Sensitive Resources
Program Director: Creating Trauma Sensitive Schools for The Attachment & Trauma Network
Special Education Director: Unity Charter School

Melissa has served as a special education teacher and a building administrator. She is currently working as a director of special education. Publicly, Dr. Sadin has been vice-president of her local School Board, is on the Board of Directors of the Attachment & Trauma Network and serves as the director of the Creating Trauma Sensitive Schools Program. She is a published author who produces numerous webinars on children with attachment trauma in schools. Currently, Dr. Sadin works as an education consultant and developmental trauma expert providing professional development to school districts, municipal service providers, and parents. As an adoptive mother, Dr. Sadin has provided first hand expertise in her work with adoptive parents at conferences and in other formal and informal settings.

Nathan Levy

Author & Consultant

President, Nathan Levy Books, LLC

Nathan Levy is the author of more than 40 books which have sold almost 250,000 copies to teachers and parents in the United States, Europe, Asia, South America, Australia and Africa. His unique <u>Stories with Holes</u> series continues to be proclaimed the most popular activity used in gifted, special education and regular classrooms by hundreds of educators. An extremely popular, dynamic speaker on thinking, writing and differentiation, Nathan is in high demand as a workshop leader in school and business settings. He has worked as a school principal, district supervisor, gifted coordinator, is a company president, parent of four daughters and management trainer. Nathan's ability to transfer knowledge and strategies to audiences through humorous, thought provoking stories assures that participants leave with a plethora of new ways to approach their future endeavors. Nathan Levy Books, LLC is pleased to be the publisher of this book.

See <u>www.storieswithholes</u> for additional offerings.

Dynamic Speakers
Creative Workshops
Relevant Topics

Nathan Levy, author of the <u>Stories with Holes</u> series and <u>There Are Those</u>, and other nationally known authors and speakers, can help your school or organization achieve positive results with children. We can work with you to provide a complete in-service package or have one of our presenters lead one of several informative and entertaining workshops.

Workshop Topics Include:

- Practical Activities for Teaching Gifted Children
- Differentiating in the Regular Classroom
- How to Help Children Read, Write and Think Better
- Using <u>Stories with Holes</u> and Other Thinking Activities
- Powerful Strategies to Enhance Learning
- Communicating Better in the Workplace
- How to Teach Hard to Reach Learners
- Communicating Better at School
- Adoption Competent Education
- IEP/504 Facilitation
- The Principal as an Educational Leader
  and many more…

Please write or call to receive our current catalog.
Nathan Levy Books, LLC
(732) 605-1643
NLevy103@comcast.net
www.storieswithholes.com

Ducks & Lions: Trauma Sensitive Resources
www.traumasensitive.com

Creating Trauma Sensitive schools for ALL children and the people who serve them.

- Creating Trauma Sensitive Schools - Professional Development
- Train-the-Trainer and Coaching models available
- IEP / 504 Facilitation for parents and schools
- Trauma-Informed Functional Behavior Assessment Services
- Gifted Activities that Work

Melissa Sadin – Executive Director
Melissa.sadin@gmail.com
 @melissasadin

Melissa and Nathan appreciate the Attachment & Trauma Network's support of families living with the impact of attachment disruption and childhood trauma.

ATN's Mission

At the Attachment & Trauma Network, it is our mission to:

Promote healing of traumatized children and their families through support, education and advocacy.

We Believe...

- We believe that traumatized <u>children</u> and those with attachment disorders <u>can heal</u>.
- We believe that <u>parents,</u> who are supported and taught therapeutic parenting, <u>are the best healing agents</u> of their traumatized child.
- We believe that traumatized children need <u>trauma-informed, attachment-focused therapies</u>.
- We believe that traumatized children learn best in <u>trauma-sensitive schools</u> where strategies are in place to help them feel safe, stay regulated and not be retraumatized or triggered.
- We believe that <u>providing resources</u> to the families <u>from the start</u> (once a traumatized child has been identified) is the best way to minimize crises and reduce disruptions and potential "rehoming".
- We believe that ongoing parent-to-parent <u>support is critical</u> in arming the families with strategies, tools and strength to persevere daily.
- We believe that "touching trauma at its heart" is more than a slogan...<u>it's a healing mission</u>.

We Believe in ATN.

For parents and caregivers of children with trauma-related special needs

Wholehearted,
Whole-Brained Parenting

A BOOK FOR THINKING, LOVING, AND COLORING

Adapted from Brené Brown's Wholehearted Parenting Manifesto
from *Daring Greatly* by Brené Brown

by Tiffany Sudela-Junker • Illustrations by Rian Kasner

Theo Today